P9-CQF-278

Little cat, are you as glad to have me to lie upon
as I am to feel your fur under my hand?

Amy Lowell

9 8 7 6 5 4 3 2 1
Digit on the right indicates the number of this printing.

ISBN 1–56138–635–9

Designed by Frances J. Soo Ping Chow
Edited by Christine Sweeney
Printed in the United States

The book may be ordered by mail from the publisher.
Please add $2.50 for postage and handling.
But try your bookstore first!

Running Press Book Publishers
125 South Twenty-second Street
Philadelphia, Pennsylvania 19103–4399

THE Cat NOTEBOOK

**BEING AN
ILLUSTRATED BOOK
WITH QUOTES**

Running Press
PHILADELPHIA · LONDON

Who can believe that there is no soul
behind those luminous eyes!

Théophile Gautier

With the qualities of cleanliness, discretion, affection, patience, dignity, and courage that cats have, how many of us, I ask you, would be capable of being cats?

Fernand Méry

The smallest feline is a masterpiece.

Leonardo da Vinci

A cat is an example of sophistication minus civilization.

Anonymous

It is with the approach of winter that cats become in a special manner our friends and guests. It is then too that they wear their richest fur and assume an air of sumptuous and delightful opulence.

Pierre Loti

Her function is to sit and be admired.

Georgina Strickland Gates

The cat is mighty dignified until
the dog comes by.

Southern folk saying

Dogs remember faces, cats places.

English saying

It is in the nature of cats to do a certain
amount of unescorted roaming.

Adlai Stevenson

In the middle of a world that has always been a bit mad,
the cat walks with confidence.

Rosanne Amberson

The cat sees through shut lids.

English saying

Cats are rather delicate creatures and they are subject to a good
many ailments, but I never heard of one who suffered from insomnia.

Joseph Wood Krutch

Cat: A pygmy lion who loves mice, hates
dogs, and patronizes human beings.

Oliver Herford

I gave an order to the cat, and
the cat gave it to its tail.

Chinese saying

A kitten is so flexible that she is almost double; the hind parts are equivalent to another kitten with which the forepart plays. She does not discover that her tail belongs to her until you tread on it.

Henry David Thoreau

No matter how much cats fight, there
always seem to be plenty of kittens.

Abraham Lincoln

A cat with kittens nearly always decides
sooner or later to move them.

Sidney Denham

Meow is like aloha—it can mean anything.

Hank Ketchum

Honest as the cat when the
meat is out of reach.

English saying

A cat is nobody's fool.

Heywood Broun

The trouble with cats is that
they've got no tact.

P. G. Wodehouse

Cats may be insecure deep down, but they never let you see it. I always love their air. They're like the man who broke the bank at Monte Carlo.

Barney Martin

There was a sound between them. A warm and contented
sound like the murmur of giant bees in a hollow tree.

Stephen Vincent Benét

All you have to remember is Rule 1: When in doubt—Wash.

Paul Gallico

He shut his eyes while Saha [the cat] kept vigil, watching all the invisible signs that hover over sleeping human beings when the light is put out.

Colette

A dog, I have always said,
is prose; a cat is a poem.

Jean Burden

At dinner time he would sit in a corner, concentrating,
and suddenly they would say, "Time to feed the cat,"
as if it were their own idea.

Lilian Jackson Braun

Cats know how to obtain food without labor, shelter
without confinement, and love without penalties.

W. L. George

Cats always know whether people like or dislike them.
They do not always care enough to do anything about it.

Winifred Carrière

The way to keep a cat is to try to chase it away.

Ed Howe

Nothing's more determined than a cat on a hot tin roof. . . .

Tennessee Williams

If you want to be a psychological novelist and write about human beings, the best thing you can do is keep a pair of cats.

Aldous Huxley

A dog is a dog, a bird is a bird, and a cat is a person.

Mugsy Peabody

A cat is there when you call her—if she
doesn't have something better to do.

Bill Adler

A cat is a tiger that is fed by hand.

Vakaoka Genrin

We cannot, without becoming cats,
perfectly understand the cat mind.

St. George Mivart

Many cats, when they are Out want to be In,
and vice versa, and often simultaneously.

Dr. Louis J. Camuti

If he had asked to have the door opened, and was eager to go out, he always went out deliberately. I can see him now, standing on the sill, looking about the sky as if he was thinking whether it were worth while to take an umbrella, until he was near to having his tail shut in.

Charles Dudley Warner

Cats know not how to pardon.

Jean de la Fontaine

A cat is a lion in a jungle of small bushes.

Indian saying

Kittens believe that all nature is occupied with their diversion.

F. A. Paradis de Moncrif

To please himself only the cat purrs.

Irish saying

Nothing's more playful than a young cat,
nor more grave than an old one.

Thomas Fuller

A kitten is chiefly remarkable for rushing about like mad at
nothing whatever, and generally stopping before it gets there.

Agnes Repplier

If he is comic, it is only because of the incongruity
of so demure a look and so wild a heart.

Alan Devoe

A cat sleeps fat, yet walks thin.

Fred Schwab

With cats one can never be certain.

Hartley and Joan Ramsay

Although all cat games have their rules and ritual, these vary with the individual player. The cat, of course, never breaks a rule. If it does not follow precedent, that simply means it has created a new rule and it is up to you to learn it quickly if you want the game to continue.

Sidney Denham

As anyone who has ever been around a cat for any length of time well knows, cats have enormous patience with the limitations of the human mind.

Cleveland Amory

As to sagacity, I should say that his judgment respecting the warmest place and the softest cushion in a room is infallible, his punctuality at meal times is admirable, and his pertinacity in jumping on people's shoulders till they give him some of the best of what is going, indicates great firmness.

Thomas Henry Huxley

The way to get on with a cat is to treat it as an equal—or even better, as the superior it knows itself to be.

Elizabeth Peters

Somebody once said that a dog looked up to a man as its superior, that a horse regarded a man as its equal, and that a cat looked down on him as its inferior.

Compton Mackenzie

There is no more intrepid explorer than a kitten.

Jules Champfleury

Cats can be very funny, and have the oddest ways of showing
they're glad to see you. Rudimace always peed in our shoes.

W. H. Auden

It is a very inconvenient habit of kittens (Alice had once made the remark) that, whatever you say to them, they always purr.

Lewis Carroll

That . . . cat purrs like a windmill, like an electric car,
like a tea-kettle, like a whole boiled dinner.

Harriet Prescott Spofford

Cats will always lie soft.

Theocritus

Cats are always ready to jump into bed.

Michael Weigall

The really great thing about cats is their endless variety. One can pick a cat to fit almost any kind of decor, color scheme, income, personality, mood. But under the fur, whatever color it may be, there still lies, essentially unchanged, one of the world's free souls.

Eric Gurney

Two things are aesthetically perfect in the world—the clock and the cat.

Emile-August Chartier

Cats are <u>always</u> elegant.

John Weitz

Watch a cat when it enters a room for the first time. It searches and smells about, it is not quiet for a moment, it trusts nothing until it has examined and made acquaintance with everything.

Jean Jacques Rousseau

Cats virtually always underestimate human intelligence
just as we, perhaps, underestimate theirs.

Roger Caras

He walked by himself, and all places were alike to him.

Rudyard Kipling

If there is one spot of sun spilling onto the
floor, a cat will find it and soak it up.

Joan Asper McIntosh

The ideal of calm exists in a sitting cat.

Jules Reynard

It is as easy to hold quicksilver between your finger
and thumb as to keep a cat who means to escape.

Andrew Lang

If a fish is the movement of water embodied, given shape,
then a cat is a diagram and pattern of subtle air.

Doris Lessing

Like a graceful vase, a cat, even
when motionless, seems to flow.

George Will

When you're special to a cat, you're special indeed . . . she brings
to you the gift of her preference of you, the sight of you, the sound
of your voice, the touch of your hand.

Leonore Fleischer

Cats love one so much—more than they will allow. But they have so much wisdom they keep it to themselves.

Mary Wilkins

If I called her she would pretend not to hear, but would come a few moments later when it could appear that she had thought of doing so first.

Arthur Weigall

Tobermory looked squarely at her for a moment and then fixed his gaze serenely on the middle distance. It was obvious that boring questions lay outside his scheme of life.

Saki

Thanks to the soothing, the bliss, that we had experienced earlier, we seemed to understand each other. We had crossed our species' boundaries and had found the common center in each other, where all creatures rest.

Elizabeth Marshall Thomas

He lives in the half-lights in secret places,
free and alone—this mysterious little great
being whom his mistress calls "My cat."

Margaret Benson

The most domesticated of cats somehow
contrives to lead an outside life of its own.

Katharine Briggs

The cat lives alone, has no need of society, obeys only when she pleases, pretends to sleep that she may see the more clearly, and scratches everything on which she can lay her paw.

François René de Chateaubriand

When a Cat adopts you there is nothing to be done about it
except to put up with it and wait until the wind changes.

T. S. Eliot

We all feel somehow released by the simple,
honest relationship with the cat.

Desmond Morris

No tame animal has lost less of its native dignity or maintained more
of its ancient reserve. The domestic cat might rebel tomorrow.

William Conway

I could half persuade myself that the word
felonious is derived from the feline temper.

Robert Southey

One reason we admire cats is for their proficiency in
one-upmanship. They always seem to come out on top,
no matter what they are doing—or pretend they do.

Barbara Webster

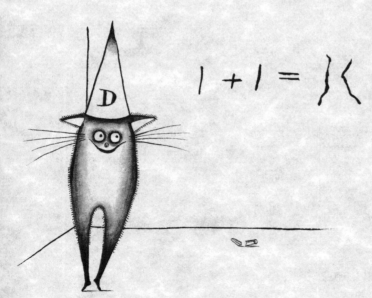

$$1 + 1 =)($$

The smart cat doesn't let on that he is.

H. G. Frommer

Human beings, for one reason or another,
may hide their feelings, but a cat does not.

Ernest Hemingway

The cat seldom interferes with other people's rights. His intelligence keeps him from doing many of the fool things that complicate life.

Carl Van Vechten

Of all domestic animals the cat is the most expressive. His face is capable of showing a wide range of expressions. His tail is a mirror of his mind. His gracefulness is surpassed only by his agility. And, along with all these, he has a sense of humor.

Walter Chandoha

It was his firm belief that I had the power to turn off the rain, brush away the clouds, make the sun come back to shine on the window ledge, modify the temperature, [and] perform other miracles as required. I found my failure to live up to his high esteem somewhat embarrassing.

Era Zistel

I called my cat William because no shorter name fits the dignity of his character. Poor old man, he has fits now, so I call him Fitz-William.

Josh Billings

If man could be crossed with the cat, it would improve man but deteriorate the cat.

Mark Twain